Charmed, I'm Sure

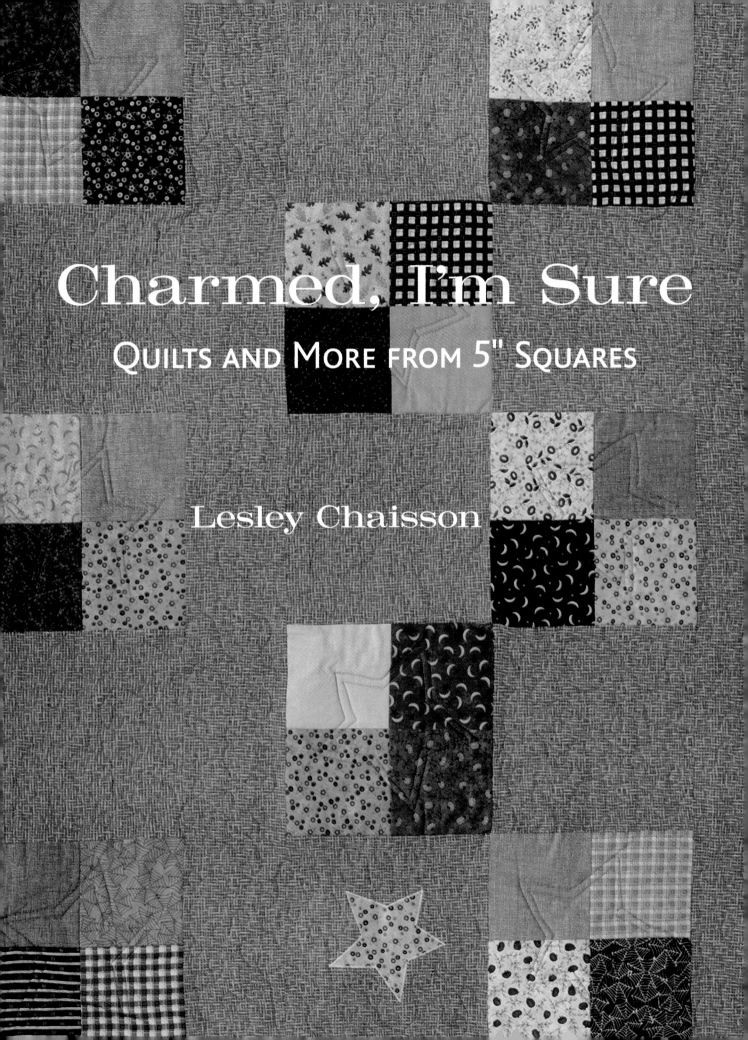

Charmed, I'm Sure

Quilts and More from 5" Squares

Lesley Chaisson

dedication

To all those who have not only the courage to use their talents, but also the willingness to share them!

acknowledgments

Many thanks to the following individuals:

My amazing children, Maranelle, Teancum, Carter, and Haylee, who are so patient not only while I worked on this book, but every time I'm in the sewing room.

My husband, Colin, who is constantly pushing me to do my best and who has been so understanding during the process of writing this book.

My parents, John and Lizz Domier, who have always given me the support and encouragement to expand my talents and the confidence to never give up.

Trena Morency, for inspiring me to quilt again and for being the most incredible quilting companion, friend, and "grandma" to my children.

Tangled Threads Quilt Guild, whose members gave me the idea to put my quilts together to create this book. They are all wonderfully talented women who continue to help me learn and inspire me to be a better quilter.

Charmed, I'm Sure: Quilts and More from 5" Squares
© 2009 by Lesley Chaisson

That Patchwork Place

Martingale®
& COMPANY

That Patchwork Place® is an imprint of Martingale & Company®.

Martingale & Company
20205 144th Ave. NE
Woodinville, WA 98072-8478 USA
www.martingale-pub.com

CREDITS

President & CEO: Tom Wierzbicki
Editor in Chief: Mary V. Green
Managing Editor: Tina Cook
Technical Editor: Ellen Pahl
Copy Editor: Marcy Heffernan
Design Director: Stan Green
Production Manager: Regina Girard
Illustrator: Laurel Strand
Cover & Text Designer: Stan Green
Photographer: Brent Kane

MISSION STATEMENT

Dedicated to providing quality products and service to inspire creativity.

Printed in China
14 13 12 11 10 09   8 7 6 5 4 3 2 1

Library of Congress Cataloging-in-Publication Data
Library of Congress Control Number: 2009013171

ISBN: 978-1-56477-901-4

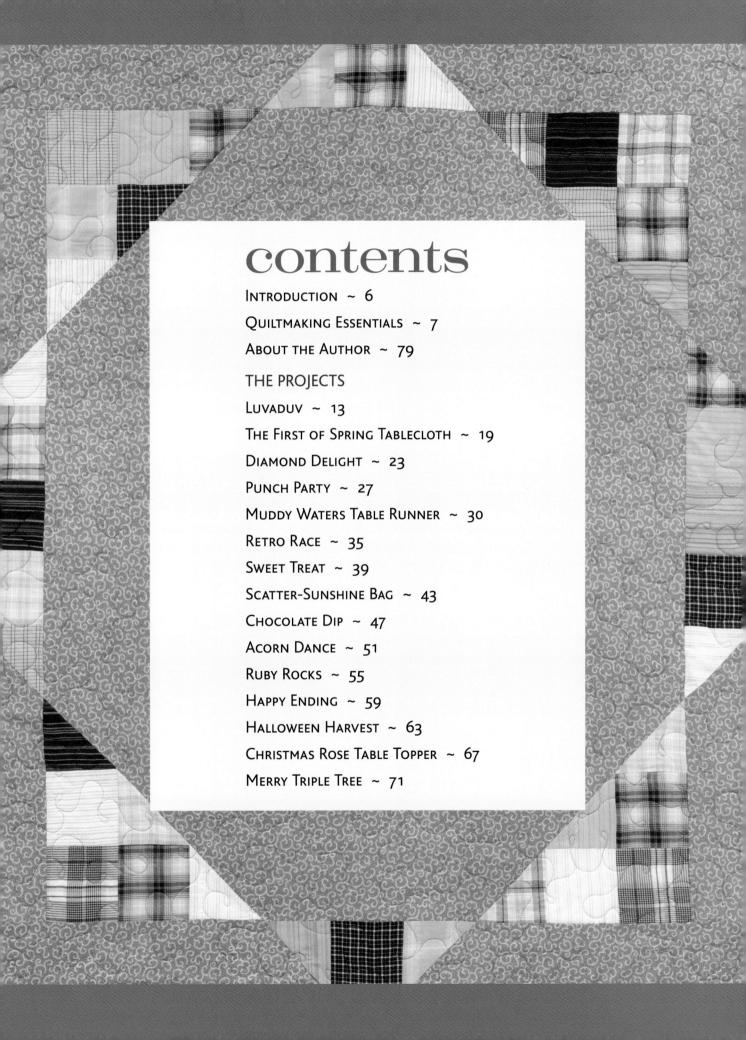

contents

introduction

This book features a new collection of fast-pieced and easy appliqué quilts, table runners, wall hangings, a tablecloth, and even a cute bag to tote around. These fun projects are perfect for the charm-square collector and simple enough for even a beginning quilter, but there are also a few more challenging ideas for a more experienced quilter.

If you're unfamiliar with charm squares, they're 5" squares of assorted fabrics, often sold in eye-catching stacks or bundles. They offer a fun way to incorporate lots of different fabrics into a quilt without needing a big stash of fabric to draw on. Many of the quilts in this book showcase the charm squares, making them the center of attention as they are without having to cut them into smaller pieces. Don't have any charm squares? No problem! Just cut 5" squares from your stash or use up scraps you just haven't been able to part with.

With easy-to-follow instructions and a little imagination, you can experiment with blocks and borders to create a quilt all your own. You won't have to spend a lot of time finding just the right fabrics for the projects—a couple of packs of precut charm squares and one or two coordinating fabrics are all you'll need. So grab a pack of charms or "quilter's candy," as I like to call them, and indulge in an assortment of sweet projects perfect for any home!

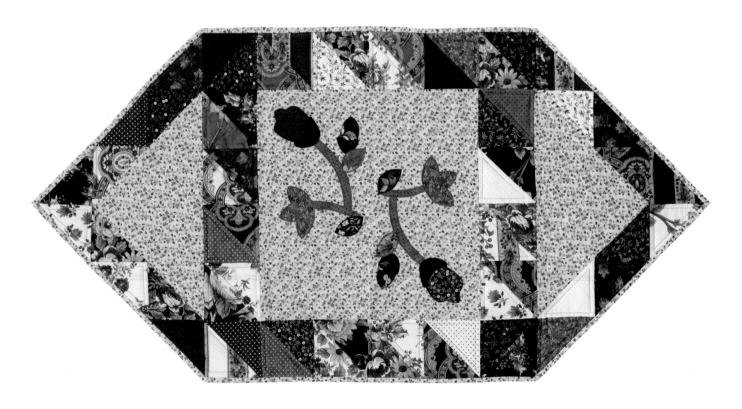

quiltmaking essentials

In this section I've included the basic techniques you'll need to make the quilts in this book. If you're a beginner and need more information, consult the staff at your local quilt shop and consider taking a class. There are also many good books on quiltmaking that you can refer to for additional guidance.

Fabric and Color Selection

I recommend using only 100%-cotton fabric because it presses crisply, holds its shape well, and maintains its color the longest. Some quilters like to prewash all their fabrics, but that is a personal preference. Just be sure to use good-quality fabric from quilt shops and other reliable sources. Do not prewash charm squares that are already cut, as the edges may ravel, leaving you with a piece that is too small.

When washing my finished quilts, I wash them in cold water with a gentle cleaner. I prefer to let them air dry. Putting them in the dryer is the fastest way to fade quilts.

Yardage requirements are provided in the materials lists for each of the projects. They are based on 42"-wide fabrics with 40" of usable fabric after prewashing. All yardages include a small margin of extra yardage to allow for minor errors and shrinkage.

CHARM SQUARE ALERT

Be aware that some charm squares may not measure exactly 5" x 5". For the patterns in this book, measure your squares first. If they are not precise, trim them to exactly 5" x 5" for best results. You may want to check the size before you buy a pack of charm squares to make sure they are cut accurately or that they are large enough to trim to the size needed.

Don't be afraid to try a color combination different from what I used in the quilts shown throughout this book. Just be sure to keep in mind the contrast needed in your project. Contrast is key in defining the design in your quilts.

Feel free to mix and match the appliqué templates with different quilts as well. For example, instead of acorns on "Acorn Dance," try the flower appliqués used on "The First of Spring Tablecloth." For any variations that you choose, just make sure you have enough charm squares or scraps to complete the quilt. Use your imagination and have fun with your candy!

Pressing

There is a difference between ironing and pressing. Ironing is when the iron is dragged across the fabric to flatten it. Pressing is the technique used most in quilting because it is less likely to distort and pull the pieces and the seams. To press, gently set the iron down onto the fabric or sewn pieces and apply pressure.

Press each seam after it is sewn. I lower my ironing board to fit under my sewing table so that I can sew a seam, and then turn to press it. If you remove any stitching to resew a seam, be sure to press the pieces so the fabrics are nice and flat again.

When working with half-square-triangle units, press the seam as it was sewn; then press the seam allowance toward the darker fabric by lowering the iron onto the seam allowance and pressing.

Cutting

Instructions for rotary cutting are given with each project. All measurements include ¼"-wide seam allowances. Any template patterns used for machine piecing have the ¼" seam allowance included.

1. Fold your fabric, aligning the selvage edges. Place the fabric on the cutting mat with the folded edge closest to you. Place a square ruler such as a Bias Square® even with the fold. Position a 6" x 24" ruler along the left side of the square ruler so that the long ruler covers the raw edges of the fabric. Remove the square ruler. Hold the long ruler firmly with your left hand and rotary cut along the right edge, removing the uneven raw edges. Always be sure to cut *away* from yourself.

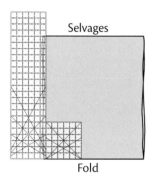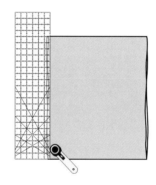

Selvages

Fold

2. To cut a strip, align the appropriate marking on the long ruler with the straight edge of the fabric. If you need a 3"-wide strip, place the 3" line on your ruler exactly on the edge of the fabric. Use your rotary cutter along the edge of the ruler to make the cut.

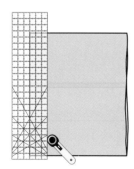

3. To cut squares or rectangles, first cut strips to the needed width. Remove the selvage ends, creating a straight edge. Align the left edge of the strips with the desired line on your ruler. Cut the strip into squares or rectangles until you have the number that you need.

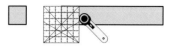

Machine Piecing

Always maintain a consistent ¼" seam allowance when sewing. Check your seam allowance and the size of your finished pieces to make sure they are accurate. Some machines have a special ¼" presser foot. You can use the edge of this foot as a guide, or you can create your own guide by placing tape or moleskin ¼" from the needle.

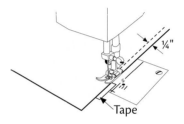

¼"

Tape

Scrappy Half-Square-Triangle Units

There are several methods for making half-square-triangle units. I typically cut squares as required, and then cut the squares in half to make triangles. I mix and match the triangles when sewing them together. This enables me to get a scrappy look with random or varied pairings of triangles. Layer the triangles right sides together, sew, press toward the darker fabric, and then trim the tiny triangles called dog-ears that extend at the corners.

PAIRED HALF-SQUARE-TRIANGLE UNITS

This method involves layering two squares and sewing them together before cutting. It will result in two identical half-square-triangle units.

1. Place the two squares that you want to pair right sides together. Draw a line diagonally from corner to corner on the wrong side of the lighter square. Sew ¼" away on both sides of the drawn line.

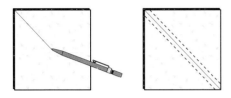

2. Cut on the drawn line. Press the seam allowances toward the darker fabric or as directed in the quilt project instructions. Trim the dog-ears.

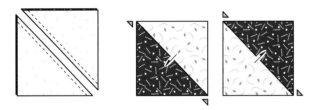

3. To trim the half-square-triangle units to the correct unfinished size, place the diagonal line of a square ruler on the seam line of the triangle square and trim the right and top sides as shown. Rotate the block and trim the remaining two sides.

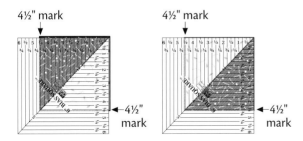

Appliqué Instructions

All the appliqué in this book is done with fusible web and the edges are stitched by machine with a satin stitch or blanket stitch. Stitch other lines on the pattern (such as the smiles of the fish in "Muddy Waters Table Runner") with a satin stitch to give good definition. Template patterns are printed at finished size for machine appliqué and in reverse for fusible web. If you plan to hand appliqué, you will need to reverse the pattern and add a seam allowance when cutting out the appliqués.

1. Trace the appliqué template onto the paper side of the fusible web. Cut out the shape, adding from ⅛" to ¼" around the traced line.

2. Press the fusible web to the wrong side of the chosen fabric, following the manufacturer's instructions. Allow to cool. Cut on the lines and peel the paper backing away from the web.

3. Position the appliqué pieces on the quilt where desired and press them into place.

4. Machine stitch around the pieces using your preferred stitch: a satin stitch, zigzag stitch, or blanket stitch.

Adding Borders

For most of the quilts in this book, I don't give exact measurements for cutting borders. It's always best to measure the quilt first. To determine how long to cut the border strips, measure the quilt top through the center in both directions, as the edges may have stretched during construction. This will ensure that the finished quilt will be as straight and as square as possible without rippling borders.

Many of the quilts in this book don't have borders, and those that do have simple butted borders. These strips generally are cut along the crosswise grain and pieced when borders are longer than 40". Some projects have you cut borders lengthwise to avoid piecing them.

1. Measure the length of the quilt through the center. Cut border strips to that measurement, piecing as necessary. Find the middle of the

borders and quilt by folding them in half and creasing to mark the centers. Pin the border strips to the sides of the quilt, matching the center and ends. Pin, easing as necessary. Sew the borders to the quilt. Press the seam allowances toward the border strips.

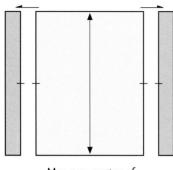

Measure center of
quilt, top to bottom.
Mark centers.

2. Measure the width of the quilt through the center, including the side borders. Cut border strips to that measurement, piecing as necessary. Mark and match the centers of the quilt and border strips as you did before. Pin and sew the borders to the top and bottom of the quilt. Press the seam allowances toward the border strips.

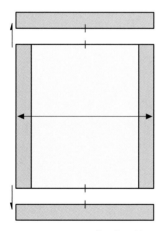

Measure center of quilt, side to
side, including border strips.
Mark centers.

Layering, Basting, and Quilting

To complete the quilt, cut and piece backing fabric to measure 2" to 4" larger than the quilt top on all sides. Place the backing right side down, layer with batting and then the quilt top, right side up. Baste with thread for hand quilting; pin with safety pins for machine quilting. Quilt by hand or machine as you desire. I enjoy my long-arm quilting machine and prefer to machine quilt all my quilts. When finished, trim the batting and backing even with the quilt top.

Binding

I cut all my bindings on the straight grain of the fabric, 2½" wide. This will result in a finished binding approximately ⅜" wide. The number of strips to cut is given in the instructions for each quilt. Join the strips with diagonal seams if you wish; I use a straight seam so that there is less bubbling on the edge of the quilt.

1. Fold the strip in half lengthwise, wrong sides together, and press.

2. Begin on one side of the quilt, aligning the raw edges of the binding with the edge of the quilt top. Leaving a 6" tail unstitched, sew the binding to the quilt using a ¼"-wide seam allowance. Stop stitching ¼" from the corner of the quilt and backstitch. Clip the threads.

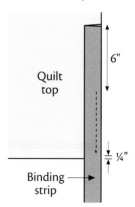

3. Position the quilt in order to sew down the next side. Fold the binding up, away from the quilt, to create a 45° angle in the fold at the corner. Fold the binding back down onto itself so that it aligns with the next edge of the quilt top. Begin stitching at the fold, backstitch, and then sew to the next corner, stopping ¼" from the edge. Repeat the folding and stitching process and continue around the quilt in this manner.

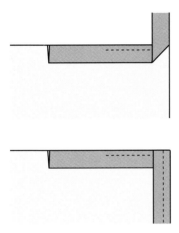

4. Stop stitching about 8" from where you began. Remove the quilt from the machine. Fold the unsewn binding edges back so they meet in the middle. Press to make a crease in each end. Trim the binding ¼" longer than the fold lines. Unfold both ends of the binding and sew together, with right sides facing, on the creased line. Press the seam allowance open, refold the binding, and continue sewing it to the quilt.

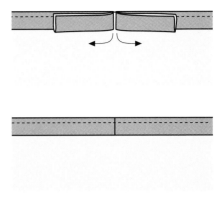

5. Fold the binding over to the back of the quilt. Hand stitch the folded edge in place, covering the machine stitching and mitering the corners.

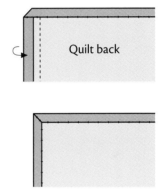

Quilt back

luvaduv

Show that special person how much you care with this cute lap quilt. Everywhere they take it they will remember how much you "luv" them!

Finished lap quilt: 51" x 60"

Materials
Yardage is based on 42"-wide fabric.
50 assorted 5" charm squares
1⅞ yards of teal fabric for inner and outer borders
1⅓ yards of light green fabric for center and binding
3⅛ yards of fabric for backing
55" x 64" piece of batting
15" x 20" piece of fusible web

Cutting
Before you cut charm squares, pick out 10 you would like for the center heart. Set these aside. All measurements include ¼"-wide seam allowances.

From *each of 20* of the charm squares, cut:
1 triangle using the template on page 17; save the leftover small triangles.

From the light green fabric, cut:
1 rectangle, 27½" x 36½"
6 binding strips, 2½" x 42"

From the teal fabric, cut:
2 strips, 7¼" x 36½" on the *lengthwise* grain
2 strips, 7¼" x 41" on the *lengthwise* grain
2 strips, 5" x 50" on the *lengthwise* grain
2 strips, 5" x 42" on the *crosswise* grain

Assembling the Quilt Top
1. Sew two end units, two side units, and four corner units as shown using the charm squares and triangles cut using the template.

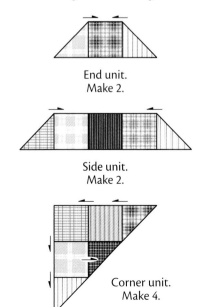

End unit.
Make 2.

Side unit.
Make 2.

Corner unit.
Make 4.

2. To make the heart, sew nine charm squares together to make a square. Sew a small leftover triangle to opposite sides of the tenth charm square, and sew this unit to the bottom of the square block.

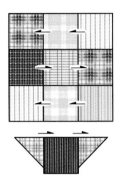

3. Make a template using the heart pattern on page 16. Referring to "Appliqué Instructions" on page 9, prepare the heart appliqué. Mark the center of the 27½" x 36½" light green rectangle by folding it in half in both directions. Center the heart on the background and fuse in place. Stitch the edges by machine.

4. Mark the swirls along the edges of the heart where indicated using the swirl pattern on page 16. Using a zigzag stitch, stitch swirls around the heart where indicated by the marks on the pattern. Sew slowly and turn the fabric with the swirl.

5. Sew the two 7¼" x 36½" teal strips to either side of the heart center. Press the seam allowances toward the center. Sew the two 7¼" x 41" teal strips to the top and bottom. Press the seam allowances toward the center.

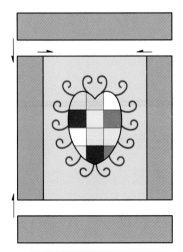

6. To add the corner units, align the 45° line of a ruler with the seam line of the green and teal fabrics as shown. Place the ¼" line at the corner and draw a line along the edge of the ruler with a pencil or other marker. Fold a corner unit in half and press lightly or pin to mark the center. Line this mark up with the corner of the heart block and align the raw edges with the drawn line. Sew ¼" from the raw edges and press toward the corner block. Trim off the excess teal fabric, leaving a ¼" seam allowance. Repeat for all corners.

45° line

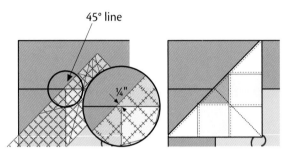

7. Cut the 5" x 42" teal strips in half at a 45° angle, cutting the strips in opposite directions. Sew one of these strips to each end of the side units as shown. Repeat for the 5" x 50" teal strips and sew them to the end units. Press the seam allowances toward the triangles.

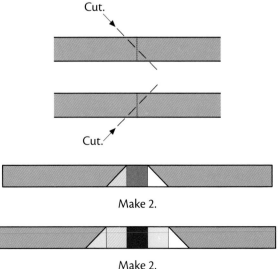

Cut.

Cut.

Make 2.

Make 2.

8. Measure the length of the quilt through the center. Divide this number in half and measure out from the center of the pieced units to cut the side borders to the correct length. To do this, fold the pieced unit in half to find the center and measure from there to trim the border strips. Sew the side borders onto the quilt, carefully matching the corners of the charm triangles. Press the seam allowances toward the outer borders. Measure the width of the quilt, including the borders just added, and repeat the process to add the top and bottom border strips.

Finishing the Quilt

Refer to "Layering, Basting, and Quilting" on page 10 as needed to finish your quilt. Join the 2½" light green strips end to end and attach the binding to your quilt, referring to "Binding" on page 10.

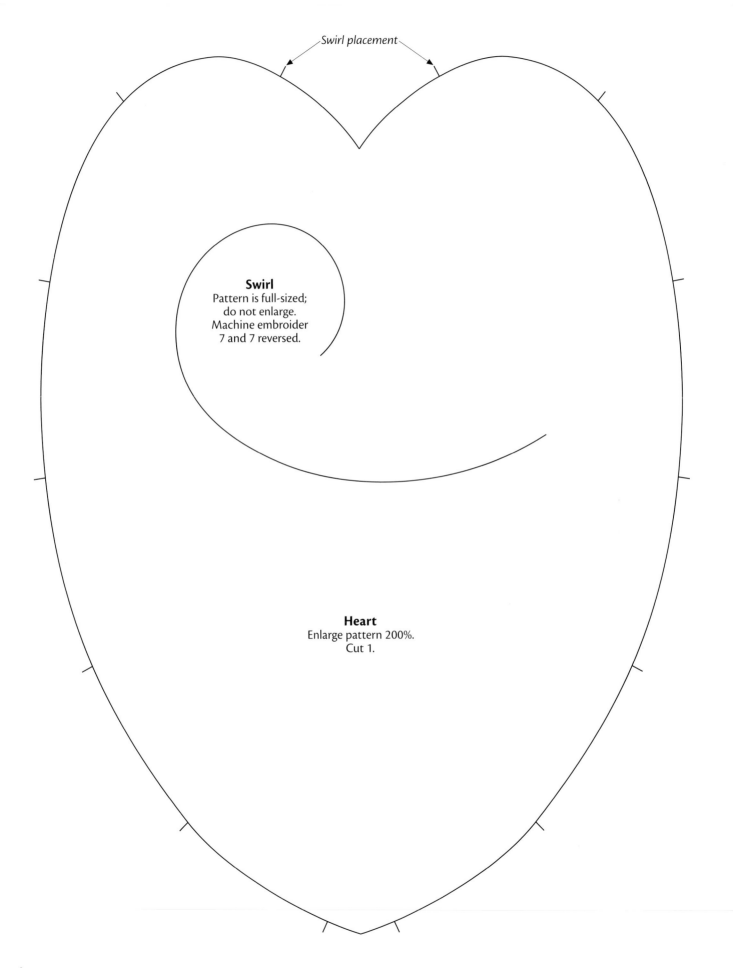

Swirl placement

Swirl
Pattern is full-sized;
do not enlarge.
Machine embroider
7 and 7 reversed.

Heart
Enlarge pattern 200%.
Cut 1.

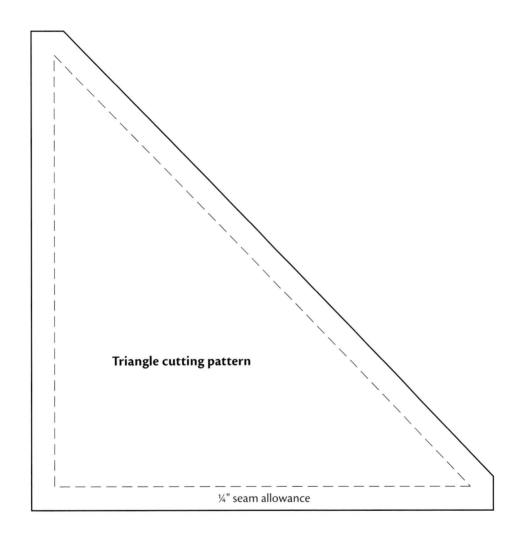

Triangle cutting pattern

¼" seam allowance

the first of spring tablecloth

A sweet and light tablecloth is perfect to welcome blooming shrubs and flowers at the beginning of spring! I made this without batting to give a light, flowing feel to the table, but it would be just as nice quilted with lovely floral motifs.

Finished quilt: 54½" x 54½"

Materials
Yardage is based on 42"-wide fabric.
60 assorted 5" charm squares for patchwork
13 assorted 5" charm squares for flower appliqués
1⅔ yards of tan fabric for flower blocks and binding
⅝ yard of green fabric for background and corners
3½ yards of fabric for backing
60" x 60" piece of batting (optional)

Cutting
All measurements include ¼"-wide seam allowances.

From the tan fabric, cut:
4 squares, 14" x 14"
1 square, 9½" x 9½"
4 rectangles, 5" x 18½"
6 binding strips, 2½" x 42"

From the green fabric, cut:
4 squares, 5" x 5"
4 rectangles, 9½" x 14"

Assembling the Tablecloth
1. Sew charm squares together as shown; press.

Make 4.

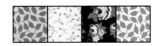

Make 4.

Make 12.

2. Sew one three-square unit from step 1 to each 14" tan square. Press the seam allowances toward the tan fabric. Then sew one four-square unit from step 1 to the bottom of each 14" square. Press the seam allowances toward the tan fabric.

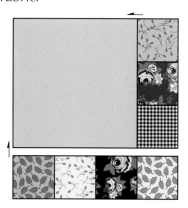

Make 4.

3. Sew a two-square unit from step 1 to one end of each 9½" x 14" green rectangle; press.

Make 4.

4. Sew a three-square unit from step 1 to both ends of the four 5" x 18½" rectangles as shown. Press toward the rectangles.

Make 4.

5. Sew 5" green squares to the ends of two of the units from step 4. Press the seam allowances toward the green squares.

Make 2.

6. Following the assembly diagram, sew the units together to make the center of the tablecloth. Press the seam allowances as indicated in the diagram.

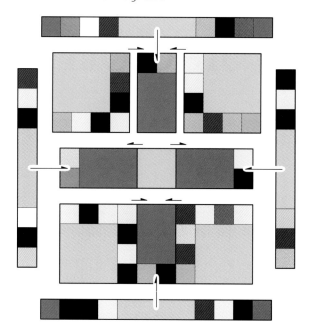

7. Make a template for the flower petal using the pattern on page 21. Use the remaining 13 charm squares and refer to "Appliqué Instructions" on page 9 to appliqué flowers to the centers of the tan squares.

DECORATIVE STITCHING

If you have decorative stitches on your sewing machine, you could use them when sewing the edges of the flower petals instead of using a satin stitch or blanket stitch. Variegated or specialty threads would be a nice touch as well.

Finishing the Tablecloth

Refer to "Layering, Basting, and Quilting" on page 10 as needed to finish your tablecloth. Batting and quilting are optional. Join the 2½" tan strips end to end and attach the binding to your tablecloth referring to "Binding" on page 10.

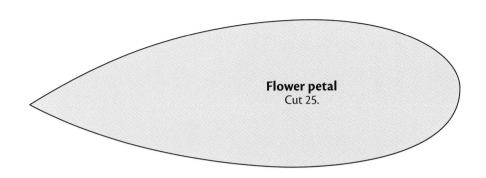

Flower petal
Cut 25.

diamond delight

This pattern is so versatile! It can be created to invoke many different moods, from elegant to festive. You can also change the values, switching the lights and darks to place light diamonds against a dark background. Or turn the diamonds on their sides, creating vertical rows of unconnected diamonds. The variations are endless!

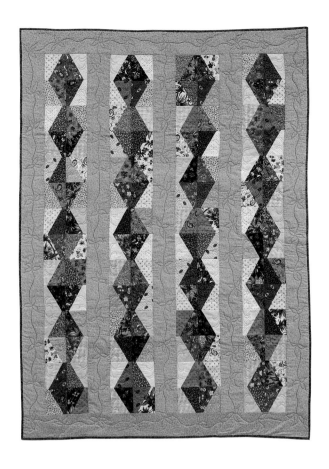

Finished quilt: 51½" x 71½"
Finished block: 7¾" x 9"

Materials
Yardage is based on 42"-wide fabric.
56 assorted light print 5" charm squares
56 assorted dark print 5" charm squares
2 yards of light brown fabric for sashing
 and borders
⅝ yard of fabric for binding
3¼ yards of fabric for backing
56" x 76" piece of batting

Cutting
All measurements include ¼"-wide seam allowances.

From the light brown fabric, cut:
5 strips, 4½" x 66", on the *lengthwise* grain
2 strips, 4½" x 54", on the *lengthwise* grain

From the binding fabric, cut:
6 strips, 2½" x 42"

CUTTING THE CHARM SQUARES
Divide the charm squares into two piles, each pile containing 28 light squares and 28 dark squares. Keep the piles separate throughout the entire cutting and sewing process.

Place a charm square on your cutting mat and measure 1" in from the left along the top edge. Make a mark on the fabric. Measure 1" in from the right along the bottom edge and make a mark. Align your ruler with the two points and cut along the diagonal. Cut one stack of charm squares in this manner. Repeat with the other stack of charm squares, but measure and cut in the opposite direction. Continue to keep the two stacks of patches separate from each other.

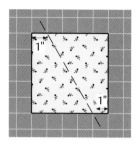

Assembling the Quilt Top

1. Sew two patches from one stack together, matching a light with a dark and making sure they are oriented as shown. Offset the points by ¼" as shown when aligning the patches. Continue until all the patches in the first stack are sewn. Press the seam allowances toward the light charm patches. Repeat to sew the patches from the second stack together; press toward the dark charm patches.

Make 56.　　　Make 56.

2. Sew one unit from each pile together to form half of the Diamond block, placing the dark patches right sides together. (Place light patches together if you want light diamonds with dark backgrounds.) Press the seam allowances in the same direction.

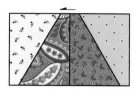

Make 56.

3. Sew the half blocks together to form the Diamond block. Make 28 blocks. Press the seam allowances to one side.

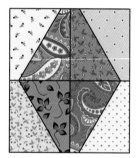

Make 28.

4. Sew seven Diamond blocks together end to end to make a vertical row; make four rows.

5. Measure the length of the diamond rows through the center. If they are different lengths, take the average and cut the five 4½" x 66" strips to that measurement. Sew these strips and the vertical diamond rows together as shown. Press the seam allowances toward the light brown strips. Referring to "Adding Borders" on page 9, measure the width of the quilt through the center. Cut and sew the remaining light brown strips to the top and bottom. Press toward the border strips.

Finishing the Quilt

Refer to "Layering, Basting, and Quilting" on page 10 as needed to finish your quilt. Join the 2½" binding strips end to end and attach the binding to your quilt, referring to "Binding" on page 10.

punch party

Arrange this lap quilt outside for a summer date on the patio. Add a glass of lemonade and a tray of freshly cut fruit—what more do you need for a perfect party?!

Finished quilt: 62¾" x 62¾"

Materials
Yardage is based on 42"-wide fabric.
99 assorted 5" charm squares*
2⅜ yards of green fabric for background
⅝ yard of peach fabric for binding
3¾ yards of fabric for backing
67" x 67" piece of batting

The instructions for this quilt use charm squares for all but the green fabric. This will result in the outer edges of the quilt being on the bias grain. If you prefer that the outer edges be on the straight grain, you will need to cut quarter-square triangles rather than half-square triangles. For this, you will need 11 squares, 7" x 7", and only 77 charm squares.

Cutting
All measurements include ¼"-wide seam allowances.

From the charm squares, cut:
99 squares once diagonally to make 198 triangles*

From the green fabric, cut:
16 strips, 4½" x 42"; cut into:
    4 rectangles, 4½" x 24½"
    4 rectangles, 4½" x 16½"
    44 rectangles, 4½" x 8½"
    8 squares, 4½" x 4½"
2 strips, 2½" x 42"; cut into:
    2 rectangles, 2½" x 12½"
    2 rectangles, 2½" x 16½"

From the peach fabric, cut:
7 binding strips, 2½" x 42"

If you prefer to use the paired method (page 9) of making half-square-triangle units resulting in a somewhat less scrappy look, do not cut 77 of the charm squares: cut only 22 squares in half to make 44 triangles for the sides. If you choose to use 11 squares, 7" x 7", cut those squares twice diagonally to make 44 quarter-square triangles for the sides.

Assembling the Quilt Top

1. Randomly select 154 charm triangles and sew them together in pairs to make 77 half-square-triangle units. Press and trim the blocks to 4½" x 4½".

2. Using the pieces as listed below, sew two of every unit (except the center unit) by following the diagrams. Press in the direction indicated by the arrows.

Corner unit 1: 6 half-square-triangle units; 10 charm triangles; 2 rectangles, 4½" x 8½"; 1 rectangle, 4½" x 16½"; 1 rectangle, 4½" x 24½"

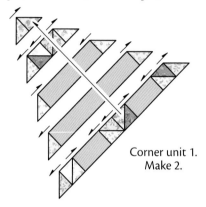

Corner unit 1.
Make 2.

Corner unit 2: 2 half-square-triangle units; 8 charm triangles; 1 rectangle, 4½" x 16½"; 1 rectangle, 4½" x 24½"

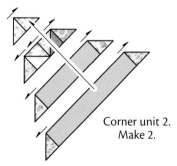

Corner unit 2.
Make 2.

Side unit 1: 6 half-square-triangle units; 2 charm triangles; 1 square, 4½" x 4½"; 5 rectangles, 4½" x 8½"

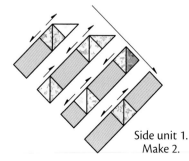

Side unit 1.
Make 2.

Rectangle unit: 8 half-square-triangle units; 2 squares, 4½" x 4½"; 5 rectangles, 4½" x 8½"

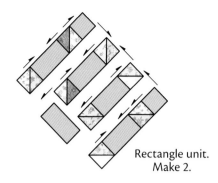

Rectangle unit.
Make 2.

Side unit 2: 6 half-square-triangle units; 2 charm triangles; 1 square, 4½" x 4½"; 5 rectangles, 4½" x 8½"

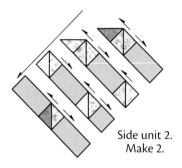

Side unit 2.
Make 2.

Square unit: 6 half-square-triangle units; 5 rectangles, 4½" x 8½"

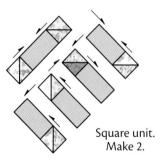

Square unit.
Make 2.

Center unit: 9 half-square-triangle units; 2 rectangles, 2½" x 12½"; 2 rectangles, 2½" x 16½"

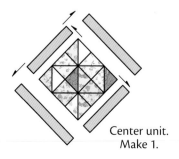

Center unit.
Make 1.

3. Follow the quilt assembly diagram to sew the side units, square units, rectangle units, and the center unit in diagonal rows. Sew the diagonal rows together. Add the corner units last. Press in the direction indicated by the arrows.

4. Trim the sides and square up the corners of the quilt, carefully handling the bias edges.

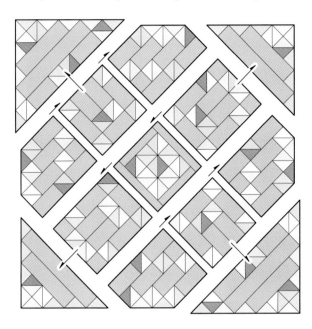

KEEP THE EDGES IN CHECK
Carefully stay stitch the outer edges of the quilt top to stabilize it before layering and basting. Stitch a scant ¼" from the raw edge on all sides, and the stitching will be hidden in the binding.

Finishing the Quilt

Refer to "Layering, Basting, and Quilting" on page 10 as needed to finish your quilt. Join the 2½" peach strips end to end and attach the binding to your quilt, referring to "Binding" on page 10.

muddy waters table runner

This cheerful table runner is fun to make. It reminds me of the way sand rises and moves in the water when you walk through it. These busy fish are moving through the water and stirring up the sand. I echo quilted around each fish to mimic ripples in the water and add a feeling of movement.

Finished quilt: 22" x 44½"
Finished block: 3¾" x 3¾"

Materials
Yardage is based on 42"-wide fabric.
40 assorted blue, tan, and cream print 5" charm squares for blocks
6 assorted tan and cream print 5" charm squares for fish
½ yard of tan print for borders
⅜ yard of blue print for binding
1½ yards of fabric for backing
26" x 49" piece of batting
12" x 17" piece of fusible web
Cutting mat with 1" grid
6 assorted buttons, ½" diameter, for fish eyes

Cutting
All measurements include ¼"-wide seam allowances.

From the tan print, cut:
2 strips, 3¾" x 22"
2 strips, 3¾" x 38"

From the blue print, cut:
4 binding strips, 2½" x 42"

Making the Blocks
1. Lay a charm square for the blocks on the cutting mat, aligning it exactly within a 5" x 5" grid. Place a ruler 3" in along the top and 1" in at the bottom; make an angled cut. This will be piece 1. Set aside.

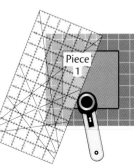

2. Place the 45° line of your ruler along the lower edge of the remaining piece as shown so that it intersects with the lower-right corner of the fabric. Make an angled cut. These will be pieces 2 and 3.

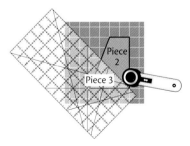

3. Repeat the cutting process with all 40 charm squares, and stack the cut patches in three piles.

4. Randomly select a piece 2 and a piece 3 from the stacks. Arrange the pieces next to each other right side up to make sure you sew the

correct side of piece 3 to piece 2. Align the pieces right sides together, offsetting the edges as shown. Sew and press the seam allowance toward piece 2. The lower edges will be uneven, but that's OK. The blocks will be trimmed later. Continue to sew pieces 2 and 3 together, making sure that you pair up different fabrics.

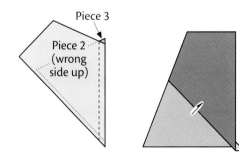

5. Sew a unit from step 4 to piece 1, offsetting the edges as shown. Press toward piece 1. Make 40 blocks.

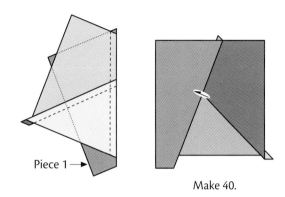

Piece 1 →

Make 40.

6. Trim and square up the blocks to measure 4¼" x 4¼".

Assembling the Table Runner

1. Sew the blocks together into 10 rows of four blocks each, pressing each row in alternating directions. Sew the 10 rows together; press.

2. Sew a 3¾" x 38" tan border strip to each long side of the table runner. Press the seam allowances toward the border.

3. Sew a 3¾" x 22" tan border strip to the remaining sides. Press the seam allowances toward the border.

4. Make a template using the fish pattern on page 33. Using the six charm squares for fish, cut and prepare the fish appliqués. Refer to "Appliqué Instructions" on page 9 and appliqué the fish to the table runner. Add the buttons for the fish eyes.

Finishing the Table Runner

Refer to "Layering, Basting, and Quilting" on page 10 as needed to finish the table runner. Join the 2½" blue print strips end to end and attach the binding to the table runner referring to "Binding" on page 10.

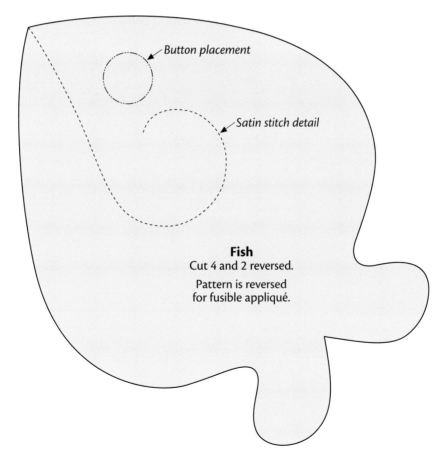

Button placement

Satin stitch detail

Fish
Cut 4 and 2 reversed.

Pattern is reversed
for fusible appliqué.

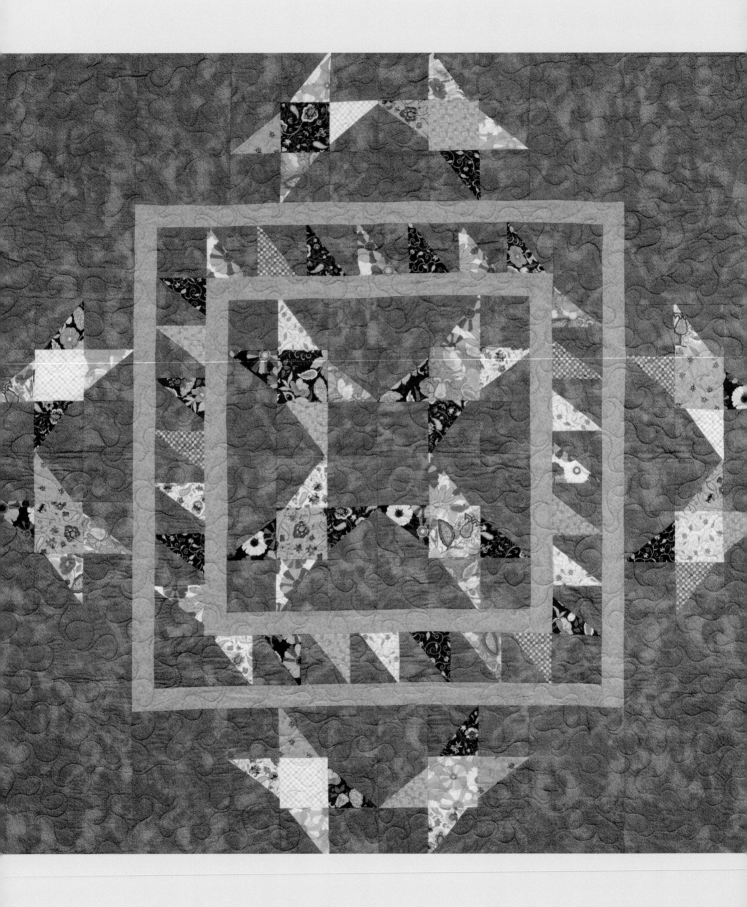

retro race

This hot pink quilt accented with trendy retro prints and colors will brighten up any room. It's tailor-made for a tween or a teenager, and it's quick and easy to cut and piece, so you will be finished in almost no time at all.

Finished quilt: 72½" x 72½"

Materials
Yardage is based on 42"-wide fabric.
50 assorted 5" charm squares
4 yards of dark pink fabric for background
1⅜ yards of light pink fabric for inner borders and binding
4½ yards of fabric for backing
77" x 77" piece of batting

Cut 38.   Cut 38 reversed.

Cutting guide

Cutting
Select 12 charm squares to be used for the center of the blocks. They are not to be cut, so set them aside for later. All measurements include ¼"-wide seam allowances.

From the dark pink fabric, cut:
10 strips, 5" x 42"; cut 38 pieces and 38 reversed using the template pattern on page 37 (Refer to the cutting guide at right.)
7 strips, 5" x 42"; cut into 52 squares, 5" x 5"
4 strips, 14" x 42"; cut into:
    4 rectangles, 14" x 23"
    4 rectangles, 9" x 14"

From the light pink fabric cut:
9 strips, 2¾" x 42"; cut 4 strips into:
    2 strips, 2¾" x 27½"
    2 strips, 2¾" x 32"
8 binding strips, 2½" x 42"

CUTTING THE CHARM SQUARES
Place a charm square on your cutting mat and measure in ¾" from the left along the top edge. Make a mark on the fabric. Measure in ¾" from the right along the bottom edge and make a mark. Align your ruler with the two points and cut along the diagonal. Cut 19 charm squares in this manner. Repeat with the other 19 charm squares, but measure and cut in the opposite direction. Keep the patches in two separate stacks.

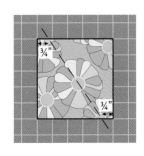
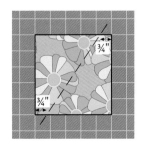

Assembling the Quilt Top

1. Arrange the cut charm patches and dark pink patches as shown. Sew together in pairs, offsetting the corners by ¼". When pressed, the straight edges should meet to make a 5" angle-pieced square. Press the seam allowances toward the charm patches. Make 38 of each.

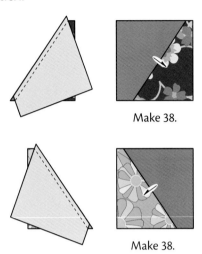

Make 38.

Make 38.

2. Sew four 5" dark pink squares, one of the set-aside 5" charm squares, and four of the angle-pieced squares just made (two of each direction) into rows as shown. Press the seam allowances toward the unpieced squares. Join the rows to make a block. Make 12. They will measure 14" x 14".

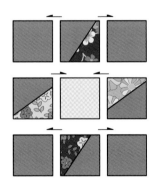

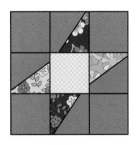

Make 12.

3. Sew together seven of the angle-pieced squares with angles slanting in the same direction to form a row. Make two rows slanting to the left and two rows slanting to the right. Press the seam allowances in one direction. On opposite ends of the rows slanting to the right, sew a 5" dark pink square. Press toward the corner squares.

Make 2.

Make 2.

4. Sew four of the blocks made in step 2 together for the center, positioning the blocks so that they form an X. Sew a 2¾" x 27½" light pink strip to the sides of the center block. Press the seam allowances toward the light pink strips. Sew a 2¾" x 32" light pink strip to the top and bottom and press.

5. Sew the rows from step 3 without corner squares to the sides of the center unit. Press the seam allowances toward the light pink strips. Sew the rows with corner squares to the top and bottom. Press toward the light pink strips.

6. Sew another set of 2¾"-wide light pink strips around the center unit, first to the sides, and then the top and bottom, referring to "Adding Borders" on page 9. Piece the strips as needed. Press the seam allowances toward the light pink strips.

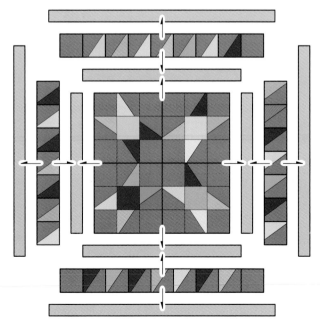

7. Sew the remaining blocks from step 2 together in pairs as shown. Sew the 9½" x 14" pink rectangles to opposite ends of two units and the 14" x 23" rectangles to opposite ends of the other two units. Press toward the rectangles.

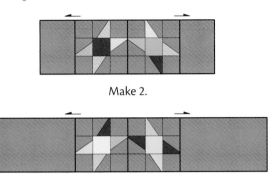

Make 2.

Make 2.

8. Sew the shorter border units to the sides first, and then sew the longer border units to the top and bottom. Press the seam allowances toward the light pink strips.

Finishing the Quilt
Refer to "Layering, Basting, and Quilting" on page 10 as needed to finish your quilt. Join the 2½" light pink strips end to end and attach the binding to your quilt, referring to "Binding" on page 10.

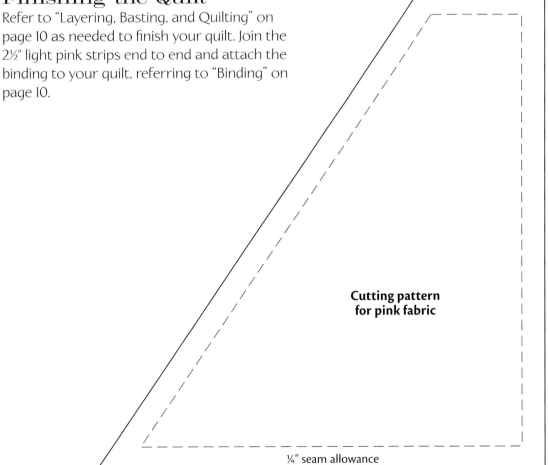

**Cutting pattern
for pink fabric**

¼" seam allowance

sweet treat

This quilt is a fantastic way to show off your quilt candy or use up favorite scraps that you just haven't been able to throw away. Note that the contrast varies within the blocks, depending on the charm-square fabric. I chose black prints for the sashing squares, because I like how they stand out.

Finished quilt: 72½" x 83"
Finished block: 8½" x 8½"

Materials

Yardage is based on 42"-wide fabric.
42 assorted 5" floral charm squares for blocks
8 assorted 5" black floral charm squares for sashing squares
3⅝ yards of plum fabric for block borders and outer border
2 yards of cream floral for sashing
⅔ yard of fabric for binding
5 yards of fabric for backing
77" x 87" piece of batting

Cutting

All measurements include ¼"-wide seam allowances.

From the plum fabric, cut:
34 strips, 2½" x 42"
8 strips, 4" x 42"

From the cream floral, cut:
26 strips, 2½" x 42"; cut 9 strips into 36 sashing rectangles, 2½" x 9"

From *each* of the 8 charm squares for sashing, cut:
4 squares, 2½" x 2½" (32 total; 2 are extra)

From the binding fabric, cut:
8 strips, 2½" x 42"

39

Assembling the Quilt Top

1. Sew 42 charm squares to 2½" x 42" plum fabric strips as shown. Cut the units apart when all the charm squares are sewn. Press the seam allowances toward the plum fabric.

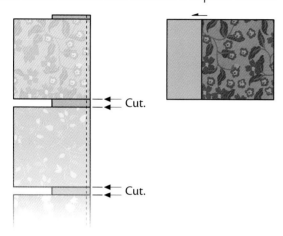

2. Sew the units from step 1 to 2½" x 42" plum strips, rotating the units 90° to add the second side. Press and cut apart as before. Continue until the charm squares are bordered by plum fabric on all four sides. Press all seam allowances toward the plum fabric. You will have 42 blocks. The side with the shortest piece is considered the top of the block.

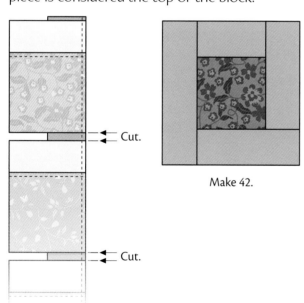

Make 42.

3. Sew a cream floral sashing strip to the right side of 35 blocks using the same method. Press the seam allowances toward the cream floral.

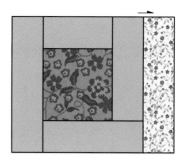

Make 35.

4. Sew five blocks from step 3 and one block from step 2 into a row, placing the block without sashing at the right end of the row. Press the seam allowances toward the sashing. Make seven rows.

Make 7.

5. Sew a 2½" square to one end of 30 of the 2½" x 9" cream floral sashing rectangles. Press the seam allowances toward the cream floral.

Make 30.

6. Sew five sashing units from step 5 into a row; add one additional 2½" x 9" sashing rectangle to the end. Press the seam allowances toward the cream floral. Make six sashing rows.

Make 6.

7. Sew the block rows together with the sashing rows as shown in the quilt assembly diagram.

8. Sew the 2½" cream floral strips together in pairs to make four long strips. Referring to "Adding Borders" on page 9, cut the strips to the correct size and sew them to the sides of the quilt. Press the seam allowances toward the cream floral. Repeat to add the cream floral strips to the top and bottom of the quilt.

9. Sew the 4" x 42" plum strips together in pairs and add them to the quilt as you did the border strips in step 8. Press the seam allowances toward the plum borders.

Finishing the Quilt
Refer to "Layering, Basting, and Quilting" on page 10 as needed to finish your quilt. Join the 2½" binding strips end to end and attach the binding to your quilt, referring to "Binding" on page 10.

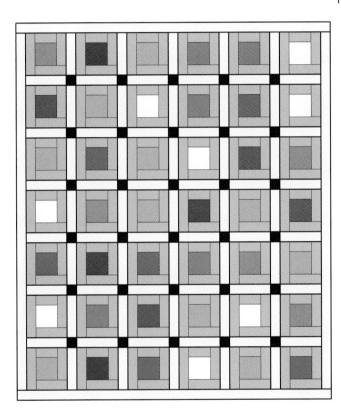

scatter-sunshine bag

With appliquéd rays of sunshine, this bag is bound to brighten your day! Or you can make it as a gift to brighten someone else's day.

Finished bag: 12" x 12" x 3"

Materials
Yardage is based on 42"-wide fabric.
20 assorted yellow 5" charm squares
20 assorted blue 5" charm squares
½ yard of fabric for lining
15" x 36" piece of batting
2½" x 40" piece of batting for handle
One 12" blue zipper
4 yards of ¼"-wide fusible web such as
   Steam-a-Seam

BEFORE YOU BEGIN
Select six yellow charm squares that you would like to use for the sunrays and eight yellow charm squares for the sun.

Assembling the Bag
1. Randomly pair up two blue charm squares right sides together. Sew along two opposite sides as shown using a ¼" seam allowance. Measure 2½" from the left raw edge with a ruler and cut in half with a rotary cutter. Repeat until you have four blue charm squares remaining.

Cut.

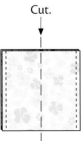

2. Repeat step 1 to sew the eight yellow charm squares for the sun together.

3. Sew the blue and yellow units together in rows. Sew one row with eight blue units and two rows with four blue and four yellow units as shown. Press the seam allowances in opposite directions from row to row. Sew the rows together and press. Repeat to make a second pieced unit, but reverse the bottom two rows so that the yellow section is on the right. One of these pieced units will be the front of the bag, and one will be the back.

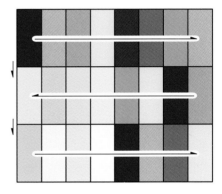

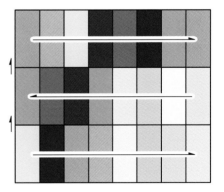

4. Draw a line down the center on the wrong side of three of the yellow charm squares set aside for the sunrays. Pair up the marked yellow charm squares, right sides together, with the other three charm squares for the sunrays. Sew along opposite edges as before and sew ¼" away on both sides of the drawn line. Cut the units apart on the drawn line and cut at an angle ¼" in from the sewn edges. Press the seam allowances open or to one side. These will be the sunrays.

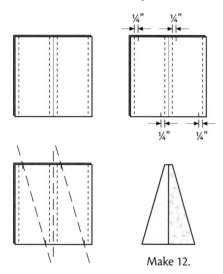

Make 12.

5. Adhere a 5" strip of the ¼"-wide fusible web to the two angled edges of each of the sunrays. Protect your ironing surface with freezer paper, scrap fabric, or an appliqué pressing sheet.

6. Position six sunrays around the yellow charm rectangles to create an arc. Overlap them as shown. When you are happy with the placement, fuse and appliqué the sunrays in place using a satin stitch and referring to "Appliqué Instructions" on page 9. I stitched a

wider satin stitch at the base of the sunrays to create the sun and a narrower stitch around the sunrays. Repeat for the second pieced unit from step 3.

7. Cut two pieces of batting, 14" x 16½". Layer the batting on the wrong side of the bag front. Baste with pins if desired and machine quilt the two layers together. Repeat for the back of the bag. Trim the edges of the batting even with the pieced front and back.

Batting →

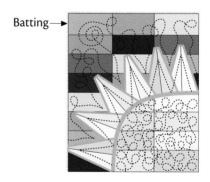

8. Follow the instructions on the zipper package to sew the zipper to the top edges of the front and back of the bag.

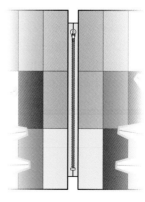

9. Cut the lining fabric into two pieces, 14" x 16½". Sew each lining piece to the bag at the zipper. Align the raw edge with the raw edge of the bag front, right sides together, at the underside of the zipper. Sew just left of the stitching line for the zipper.

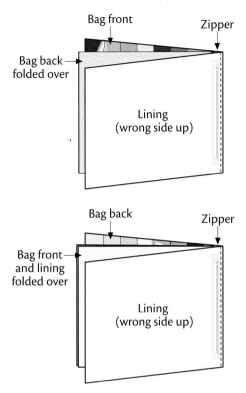

10. Fold the lining away from the zipper on the inside and topstitch ¼" from the zipper on the right side of the bag front and back. Open the zipper if needed.

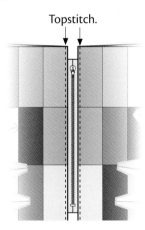

Topstitch.

11. Cut a 2" x 5" rectangle from one charm square; fold it in half right sides together and stitch using a ½" seam allowance along the raw edges. Turn right side out to make a loop for the top corner; press.

12. Open the lining so that the right sides are together and the front and back of the bag are right sides together. Insert the loop into the seam 1¾" below the zipper so that you will sew both of the raw edges into the seam. Sew on all edges using a ½" seam allowance; leave an 8" opening in the bottom of the lining.

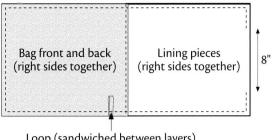

Loop (sandwiched between layers)

13. Sew the nine remaining charm squares together end to end to form the handle; press the seam allowances in one direction. Fold the strip in half lengthwise right sides together and lay the 2½" x 40" piece of batting on top. Sew using a ½" seam allowance along one long edge. Trim the batting close to the stitching and turn the handle inside out. Topstitch ¼" from each side of the handle.

14. Insert the handle through the loop. Pin one end at the bottom corner of the bag, on the same side as the loop. Pin the other end at the top corner, next to the zipper at the opposite end of the loop. Make sure that the handle is flat and not twisted.

15. Fold the bottom corner without the handle as shown; sew 3" across the corner. Repeat at the opposite bottom corner, sandwiching the end of the handle in the seam. Repeat for the lining and the top of the bag at the zipper. Sandwich the other end of the handle in the seam at the corner opposite the loop. Cut excess fabric from the corners, leaving a ½" seam allowance.

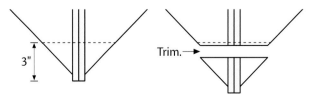

16. Turn the bag right side out, sew the opening in the lining closed, and tuck it down inside the bag.

chocolate dip

This quilt is like your favorite ice cream with colorful toppings served at the corner store—it will surely tempt you to indulge in using up those delicious charm squares! You may have to make more than one!

Finished quilt: 56½" x 72½"
Finished block: 8" x 8"

Materials
Yardage is based on 42"-wide fabric.
144 assorted 5" charm squares
3¼ yards of cream fabric for background and borders
⅝ yard of blue print for binding
3¾ yards of fabric for backing
61" x 77" piece of batting
Paper or cardstock for placement guide

Cutting
All measurements include ¼"-wide seam allowances.

From the charm squares, cut:
48 squares twice diagonally to make 192 triangles*

From the cream fabric, cut:
19 strips, 4½" x 42"; cut 12 strips into 96 squares, 4½" x 4½"

From the blue print, cut:
7 strips, 2½" x 42"

Choose colors and prints that are darker than the cream fabric so that there will be enough contrast in the X blocks.

Assembling the Quilt Top
1. Randomly select two charm squares. Layer them right sides together and sew using a ¼" seam allowance along two opposite sides as shown on the next page. Align the 2½" line of a ruler with the raw edge of the squares and cut

down the center of the square with a rotary cutter. Press the seam allowances to one side. Repeat for all 96 squares.

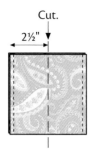

Cut.
2½"

2. Randomly select two units from step 1 with the seam allowances pressed in opposite directions. Layer the units right sides together and sew along opposite sides of the square, perpendicular to the previous seam and using a ¼" seam allowance. Cut down the center as before. Press and trim if needed. The units should measure 4½" square. You will have 96 Four Patch blocks.

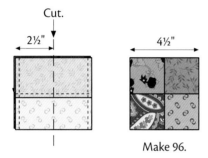

Cut.
2½"

4½"

Make 96.

3. Sew four Four Patch blocks into one larger Sixteen Patch block. Make 24 blocks. Blocks should measure 8½" square. When sewing the Four Patch blocks together, try to make sure that no two fabrics end up side by side.

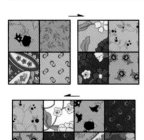

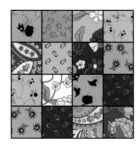

Make 24.

4. Make a placement guide from paper or cardstock using the pattern on page 49. Place the guide on a 4½" cream square, aligning the sides and corner, and align a charm triangle, wrong side up, next to it as shown. Sew along the edge of the triangle using a ¼" seam allowance. Repeat on the opposite corner of the cream square. Trim the corners, leaving a ¼" seam allowance; press. Make 96 of these units; press 48 with seam allowances toward the cream fabric and 48 with seam allowances toward the triangles. (This will help with butting the seams later.) Keep the units in two separate stacks. Handle and press these units carefully, as the two pieced corners will have bias edges.

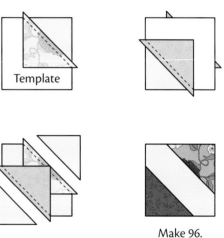

Template

Make 96.

5. Sew four of the units from step 4 together using two from each stack to make an X block. Make 24 X blocks.

Make 24.

6. Arrange the blocks into eight rows of six blocks each, alternating the Sixteen Patch blocks and the X blocks. Press the seam

allowances toward the Sixteen Patch blocks. Sew the rows together and press.

7. Sew the 4½" cream border strips together to make one long strip. Referring to "Adding Borders" on page 9, measure, trim, and sew borders onto the sides and then the top and bottom of the quilt. Press the seam allowances toward the borders.

Finishing the Quilt

Refer to "Layering, Basting, and Quilting" on page 10 as needed to finish your quilt. Join the 2½" blue print strips end to end and attach the binding to your quilt, referring to "Binding" on page 10.

Placement guide pattern

acorn dance

People always seem to love this quilt whenever I display it. I think it's due to the warm, appealing colors. The curly ribbon border really makes the acorns appear to be in motion, dancing the season away!

Finished quilt: 57½" x 57½"

Materials
Yardage is based on 42"-wide fabric.
52 assorted medium print 5" charm squares for borders
16 assorted light print 5" charm squares for center appliqué background
7 assorted 5" charm squares for appliqués
2⅛ yards of cream print for background
½ yard of fabric for binding
3½ yards of fabric for backing
62" x 62" piece of batting
12" x 18" piece of fusible web

Cutting
All measurements include ¼"-wide seam allowances.

From the medium print charm squares, cut:
24 squares once diagonally to make 48 triangles

From the cream print, cut:
5 squares, 9¼" x 9¼"; cut twice diagonally to make 20 triangles
2 strips, 2½" x 36½"
2 strips, 2½" x 40½"
3 strips, 5" x 42"; cut into:
    2 strips, 5" x 18½"
    2 strips, 5" x 27½"
6 strips, 5" x 42"

From the binding fabric, cut:
6 strips, 2½" x 42"

Assembling the Quilt Top
1. Sew the 16 light charm squares for the appliqué background into four rows of four squares; press the seam allowances in opposite directions from row to row. Sew the rows together to make the center block. Press the seam allowances in one direction.

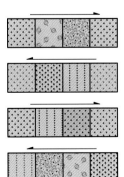
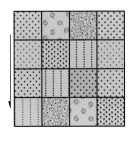

2. Sew a 5" x 18½" cream print strip to the sides of the center block. Press the seam allowances toward the cream print strips. Sew a 5" x 27½" cream print strip to the top and bottom of the center block. Press the seam allowances toward the strips.

3. Sew two rows of six charm squares; press the seam allowances in one direction. Sew the rows to the top and bottom of the center block. Press the seam allowances toward the center. Sew two rows of eight charm squares, and sew the rows to the sides of the center block.

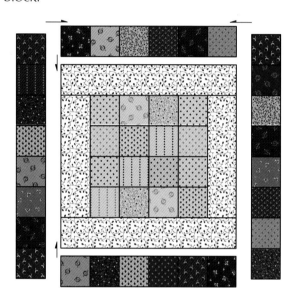

4. Sew 2½" x 36½" cream print strips to the sides of the center block; then sew 2½" x 40½" cream print strips to the top and bottom. Press the seam allowances toward the cream print.

5. Sew two charm triangles to each of the 20 triangles cut from the cream print to make flying-geese units as shown. Press the seam allowances toward the charm triangles. Trim so that the flying-geese units measure 4½" x 8½".

Make 20.

6. Sew the flying-geese units together into rows, alternating the direction of the cream print triangle. Make four rows of five flying-geese units; press.

Make 4.

7. Sew the eight remaining charm triangles together in pairs along the bias to make corner squares. Trim to 4½" x 4½". Sew one on opposite ends of two rows from step 6.

Make 2.

8. Sew the shorter rows to the sides of the quilt center and add the longer rows with the corner squares to the top and bottom. Press the seam allowances toward the cream print border.

9. Cut two of the 5" x 42" cream print strips in half to yield four equal lengths; sew one to each of the remaining four border strips. Refer to "Adding Borders" on page 9 to measure, cut, and sew the borders to the quilt. Add borders to the sides first, and then to the top and bottom. Press toward the outer borders.

10. Make templates for the acorn using the patterns below. Referring to "Applique Instructions" on page 9, appliqué acorns to the quilt center.

Finishing the Quilt

Refer to "Layering, Basting, and Quilting" on page 10 as needed to finish your quilt. Join the 2½" binding strips end to end and attach the binding to your quilt, referring to "Binding" on page 10.

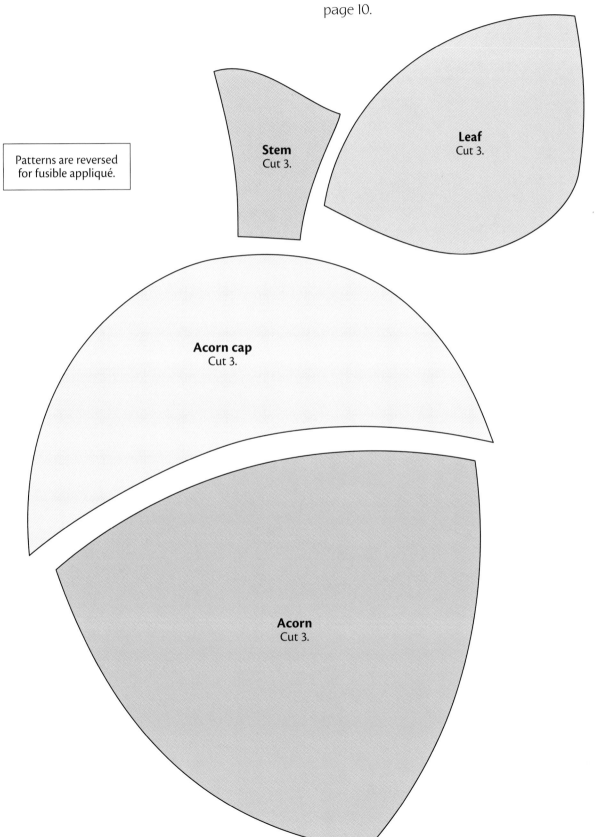

Patterns are reversed for fusible appliqué.

Stem
Cut 3.

Leaf
Cut 3.

Acorn cap
Cut 3.

Acorn
Cut 3.

ruby rocks

The charm squares in this quilt are pieced and cut so that the edges of the design appear to be cut like a gemstone. Alter the color combination to create your own gem, whether it's an emerald, sapphire, or topaz!

Finished quilt: 68" x 68"

Materials
Yardage is based on 42"-wide fabric.
108 assorted 5" charm squares
2½ yards of salmon fabric for background
⅝ yard of burgundy fabric for binding
4 yards of fabric for backing
72" x 72" piece of batting

Cutting
All measurements include ¼"-wide seam allowances.

From *each of 32* of the charm squares, cut:
1 triangle using the template on page 57

From the salmon fabric, cut:
7 strips, 5" x 42"; cut into:
    2 rectangles, 5" x 14"
    3 strips, 5" x 32"
    2 strips, 5" x 41"
    8 triangles using the template on page 57
4 squares, 14" x 14"
1 square, 32¾" x 32¾"; cut twice diagonally to make 4 triangles

From the burgundy fabric, cut:
7 strips, 2½" x 42"

Assembling the Quilt Top
Note: For easier assembly, the corners of the quilt will be constructed in a slightly different manner than the corners of the quilt shown in the photograph.

1. Randomly select nine charm squares, and sew them into rows of three to make a Nine Patch block. Make four. The blocks will measure 14" square.

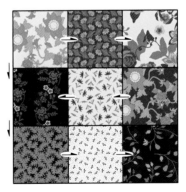

Make 4.

2. Sew a Nine Patch block to either side of a 5" x 14" salmon rectangle. Press the seam allowances toward the rectangle. Make two.

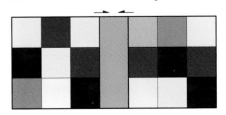

Make 2.

3. Sew a 5" x 32" salmon strip to the top and bottom of one of the units from step 2. Press the seam allowances toward the salmon fabric. Sew a 5" x 32" salmon strip to the bottom of the second unit; press. Sew the units together. Sew a 5" x 41" salmon strip to each side; press.

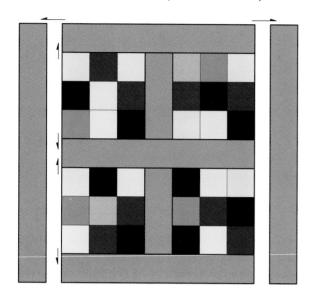

4. Sew five charm squares and four charm triangles together as shown. Sew a salmon triangle, cut using the template, to the top. Make four units slanting to the right and four slanting to the left. Press the seam allowances as indicated by the arrows in the diagram.

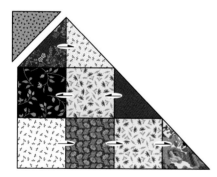

Make 4.

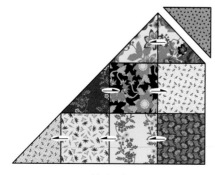

Make 4.

5. To make the border units, you need to trim the large salmon triangles. Place a ruler on the 90° corner of the large salmon triangle where it measures 4¾" across; align the 45°-angle line of the ruler with the edge of the triangle and cut off the corner.

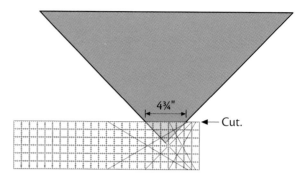

4¾" ← Cut.

6. Sew one right-slanting and one left-slanting block to the sides of the triangle, aligning them as shown. Press the seam allowances toward the salmon fabric.

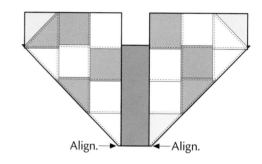

Align. ——   ——— Align.

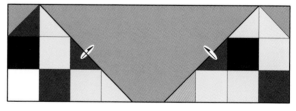

Make 4.

7. Sew a 14" salmon square to each end of a border unit made in step 6. Press the seam allowances toward the salmon fabric. Make two borders total, one each for the top and bottom of the quilt.

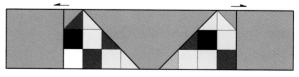

Make 2.

8. Sew the side border units to the quilt center; press. Sew the top and bottom borders with 14" squares to the quilt and press.

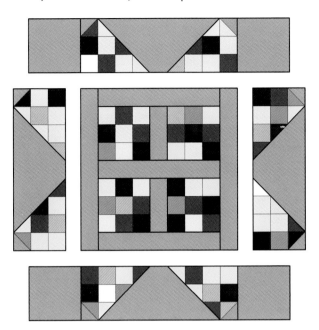

Finishing the Quilt

Refer to "Layering, Basting, and Quilting" on page 10 as needed to finish your quilt. Join the 2½" burgundy strips end to end and attach the binding to your quilt, referring to "Binding" on page 10.

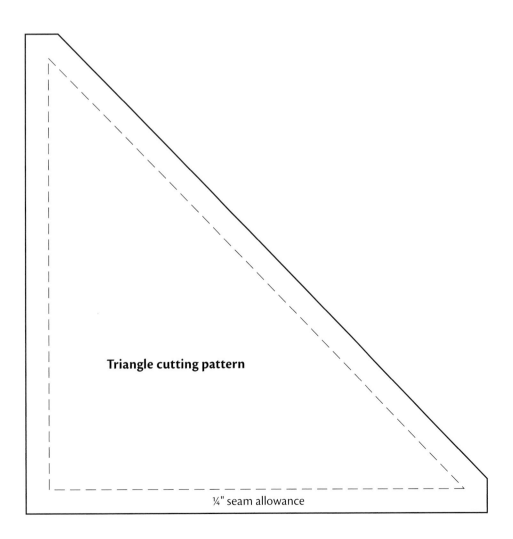

Triangle cutting pattern

¼" seam allowance

happy ending

This quilt goes together quickly and results in a fun vertical zigzag to showcase beautiful quilting designs or your favorite fabrics. Just be sure you have adequate contrast between your charm squares and the background fabric.

Finished quilt: 81½" x 105½"

Materials

Yardage is based on 42"-wide fabric.
96 assorted 5" charm squares
7¼ yards of green fabric for background and border
⅞ yard of fabric for binding
8 yards of fabric for backing
86" x 110" piece of batting

Cutting

All measurements include ¼"-wide seam allowances.

From the green fabric, cut:
12 strips, 5" x 42"; cut into 96 squares, 5" x 5"
15 strips, 8½" x 42"; cut into:
    2 rectangles, 4½" x 8½"
    19 squares, 8½" x 8½"
    20 rectangles, 8½" x 16½"
9 border strips, 5" x 42"

From the binding fabric cut:
10 strips, 2½" x 42"

Assembling the Quilt Top

1. Referring to "Paired Half-Square-Triangle Units" on page 9, make 192 half-square-triangle units with the charm squares and green fabric squares. Press the seam allowances toward the green fabric, referring to "Pressing" on page 7 for tips on how to press half-square-triangle units. Trim the units so that they measure 4½" x 4½".

2. Sew the triangle squares together in pairs to form 48 rectangles with angles slanting to the left and 48 with angles slanting to the right. Press as indicated.

Make 48 of each.

59

3. Sew a left-slanting and a right-slanting rectangle together so that the charm fabrics form a point. Press the seam allowances as shown and repeat to make 46 pieced squares. (You will have four rectangles left over, two left slanting and two right slanting.) The squares should measure 8½" x 8½".

Make 46.

4. Sew together 20 square units from step 3 to make 10 rectangles with points touching. Press the seam allowances to one side.

Make 10.

5. Sew two 8½" x 16½" rectangles to opposite sides of the 10 units from step 4 as shown. Press the seam allowances toward the green fabric.

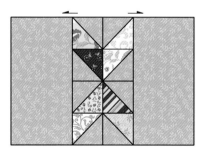

Make 10.

6. Sew a pieced square from step 3 to opposite sides of an 8½" green square, making sure the points are pointing away from the center square. Repeat to make 11 of these units.

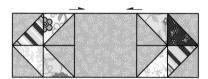

Make 11.

7. Sew 8½" green squares to opposite sides of the remaining four pieced squares from step 3. Make four.

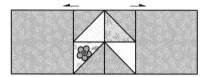

Make 4.

8. Using the remaining pieced rectangles from step 2, sew a left-slanting rectangle to one end of a 4½" x 8½" rectangle and a right-slanting rectangle to the other end as shown. Make two units.

Make 2.

9. Following the quilt assembly diagram, arrange the units to form three vertical rows. Press the seam allowances in opposite directions, and then sew the rows together.

10. Sew the 5"-wide green border strips together end to end in pairs. Cut the remaining border strip in half and add a half strip to two of the long border strips for the sides. Refer to "Adding Borders" on page 9 to measure, trim, and sew the borders to the sides, top, and bottom of the quilt.

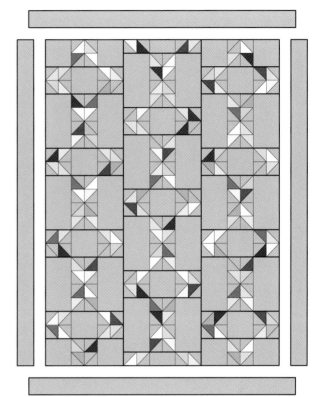

Finishing the Quilt

Refer to "Layering, Basting, and Quilting" on page 10 as needed to finish your quilt. Join the 2½" binding strips end to end and attach the binding to your quilt, referring to "Binding" on page 10.

halloween harvest

The orange and black fabrics I used in this quilt almost shout, "Trick or treat!" This simple quilt is fun to sew with any of your favorite charm squares in any color combination. Add many more stars or none at all! Either way, this quilt is something good to look at!

Finished quilt: 73" x 82"
Finished block: 9" x 9"

Materials
Yardage is based on 42"-wide fabric.
72 assorted 5" charm squares for blocks
2 different 5" charm squares for stars*
3½ yards of orange fabric for background and binding
1⅓ yards of black print for borders
5 yards of fabric for backing
77" x 86" piece of batting
5" x 12" piece of fusible web for 2 star appliqués
This quantity is based on one charm square for each star appliqué. If you want more than two stars, you will need additional charm squares.

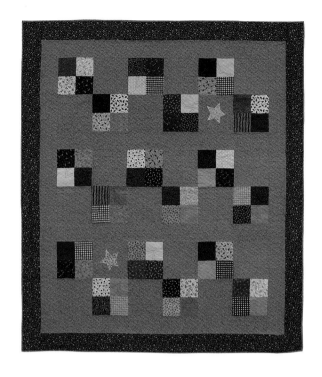

Cutting
All measurements include ¼"-wide seam allowances.

From the orange fabric, cut:
5 strips, 9½" x 42"; cut into 18 squares, 9½" x 9½"
10 strips, 5" x 42"
8 binding strips, 2½" x 42"

From the black print, cut:
8 strips, 5" x 42"

Assembling the Quilt Top

1. Sew four charm squares together to make a Four Patch block. Press the seam allowances in the direction of the arrows. Make 18 blocks.

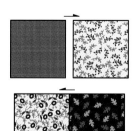 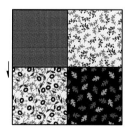

Make 18.

2. Sew one 9½" orange square to each Four Patch block. Press the seam allowances toward the orange square.

3. Sew six of the units from step 2 together, alternating the position of the orange squares. Make three rows; press.

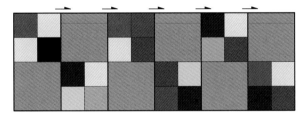

Make 3.

4. Cut one 5"-wide orange strip in half and sew a half strip to each of two 5" x 42" orange strips for sashing between rows. Measure the length of the three rows from step 3 and cut the sashing strips to the measured length. They should measure 54½". Sew the rows and sashing strips together. Press the seam allowances toward the orange fabric.

5. For the orange border, cut one 5" orange strip in half and sew a half strip to each of two 5" x 42" orange strips as before. Cut these strips to the measured length from step 4 and sew them to the top and bottom of the quilt; press.

6. Sew the remaining four 5" x 42" orange strips together in pairs for the side borders. Measure your quilt, referring to "Adding Borders" on page 9. Cut the border strips to the measured length and sew them to the sides. Press the seam allowances toward the orange borders.

7. Sew the black print border strips together into one long length. Repeat the measuring process and sew strips to the top and bottom first, and then sew strips to the sides. Press the seam allowances toward the black print.

8. Make a template for the star using the pattern on page 65. Referring to "Appliqué Instructions" on page 9 and using the remaining charm squares, appliqué stars to the quilt.

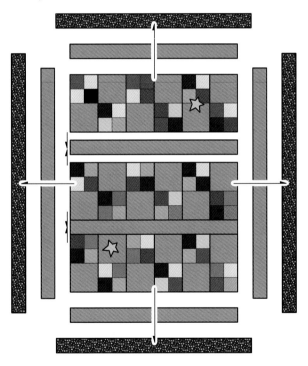

Finishing the Quilt

Refer to "Layering, Basting, and Quilting" on page 10 as needed to finish your quilt. Join the 2½" orange strips end to end and attach the binding to your quilt, referring to "Binding" on page 10.

Star
Cut 2.

Pattern is reversed
for fusible appliqué.

christmas rose table topper

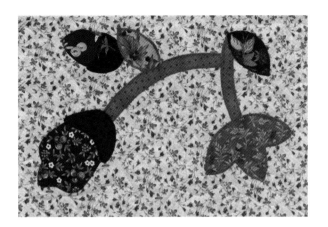

Sweet, simple flower buds are a perfect welcome for the holidays. Green and red are a classic color combination, so you can leave this table topper out year-round as well. Or make a second one in your choice of festive colors to celebrate another occasion.

Finished table topper: 25" x 50"

Materials
Yardage is based on 42"-wide fabric.
30 assorted 5" charm squares for patchwork
6 assorted 5" charm squares for appliqués
⅞ yard of cream floral for center and binding
1⅔ yards of fabric for backing
29" x 54" piece of batting
12" x 15" piece of fusible web

Cutting
All measurements include ¼"-wide seam allowances.

From the charm squares for patchwork, cut:
30 squares once diagonally to make 60 triangles

From the cream floral, cut:
1 square, 12½" x 12½"; cut once diagonally to make 2 triangles
1 square, 17" x 17"
4 binding strips, 2½" x 42"

Assembling the Quilt Top
1. Randomly sew 40 charm triangles together along the bias to make 20 half-square-triangle units. Press the seam allowances to one side.

2. Sew the half-square-triangle units into four strips, two with four squares each and two with six squares each. Press the seam allowances in one direction.

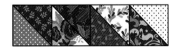

Make 2.

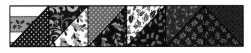

Make 2.

3. Sew two charm triangles together along the short edges, as shown; make four slanting to the right and four slanting to the left.

Make 4 of each.

4. Sew two charm triangles together along the short edges to form a larger triangle as shown. Make two.

Make 2.

5. Sew the shorter half-square-triangle strips onto the sides of the 17" cream floral square. Then sew the longer strips to the top and bottom. Press the seam allowances toward the center square.

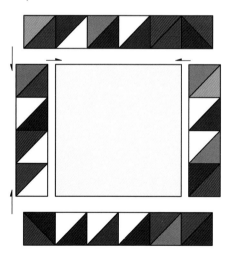

6. Make templates using the patterns on page 69. Referring to "Appliqué Instructions" on page 9 and using the remaining charm

squares, prepare and appliqué the flowers, stems, and leaves to the cream floral center.

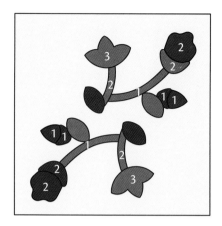

7. Sew the remaining charm-triangle units to the cream print triangles as shown. Press the seam allowances toward the cream print triangles. Sew the units to the center to complete the table topper.

Finishing the Table Topper

Refer to "Layering, Basting, and Quilting" on page 10 as needed to finish your topper. Join the 2½" cream floral strips end to end and attach the binding to your topper, referring to "Binding" on page 10.

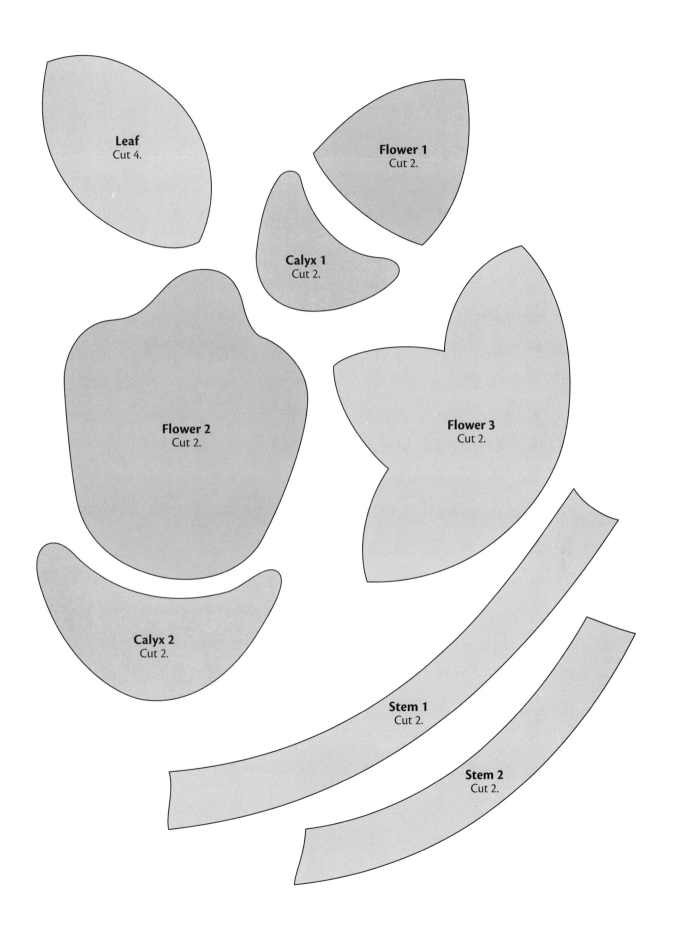

Leaf
Cut 4.

Flower 1
Cut 2.

Calyx 1
Cut 2.

Flower 2
Cut 2.

Flower 3
Cut 2.

Calyx 2
Cut 2.

Stem 1
Cut 2.

Stem 2
Cut 2.

merry triple tree

These charming trees create a smart yet sophisticated look to add to your seasonal decor. Hang this quilt on a wall, or use it on a table topped with a bowl filled with sparkly round Christmas ornaments.

Finished quilt: 45½" x 45½"

Materials
Yardage is based on 42"-wide fabric.
64 assorted medium to dark 5" charm squares
36 assorted light 5" charm squares
1 brown print 5" charm square for tree trunks
2 different green fat quarters for trees
½ yard of fabric for binding
2⅞ yards of fabric for backing
50" x 50" piece of batting
1¼ yards (12" wide) of fusible web

CHARM SQUARE CHOICES
If you find that your charm pack has more darks than needed, you can position them so that they will be behind the trees where they won't show. You can also change the values and use 36 dark and 64 light charm squares with lighter green fabrics for the trees.

Cutting
All measurements include ¼"-wide seam allowances.

From the binding fabric, cut:
5 strips, 2½" x 42"

Assembling the Quilt Top
1. Sew the 36 light charm squares into six rows of six squares each. Press the seam allowances in opposite directions from row to row.

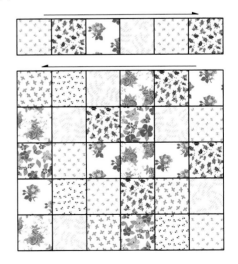

2. Sew 10 dark charm squares together to make a row. Make four rows. Press the seam allowances in opposite directions from row to row. Sew the rows together in pairs.

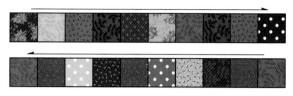

Make 2 of each.

3. Sew six dark charm squares together into a row. Make four rows. Press the seam allowances in opposite directions from row to row. Sew the rows together in pairs.

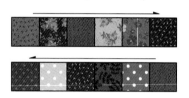

Make 2 of each.

4. Using the patterns on pages 73–77, make templates for the trees and trunks. Prepare and appliqué the trees and trunks to the light center, referring to "Appliqué Instructions" on page 9 and using the two green fat quarters and the brown print charm square.

5. Assemble the units together, adding the shorter rows to the sides and the longer rows to the top and bottom.

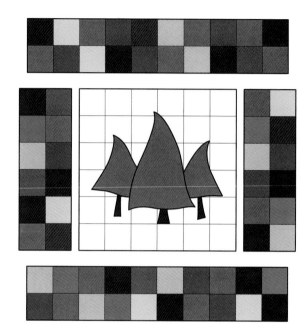

Finishing the Quilt

Refer to "Layering, Basting, and Quilting" on page 10 as needed to finish your quilt. Join the 2½" binding strips end to end and attach the binding to your quilt, referring to "Binding" on page 10.

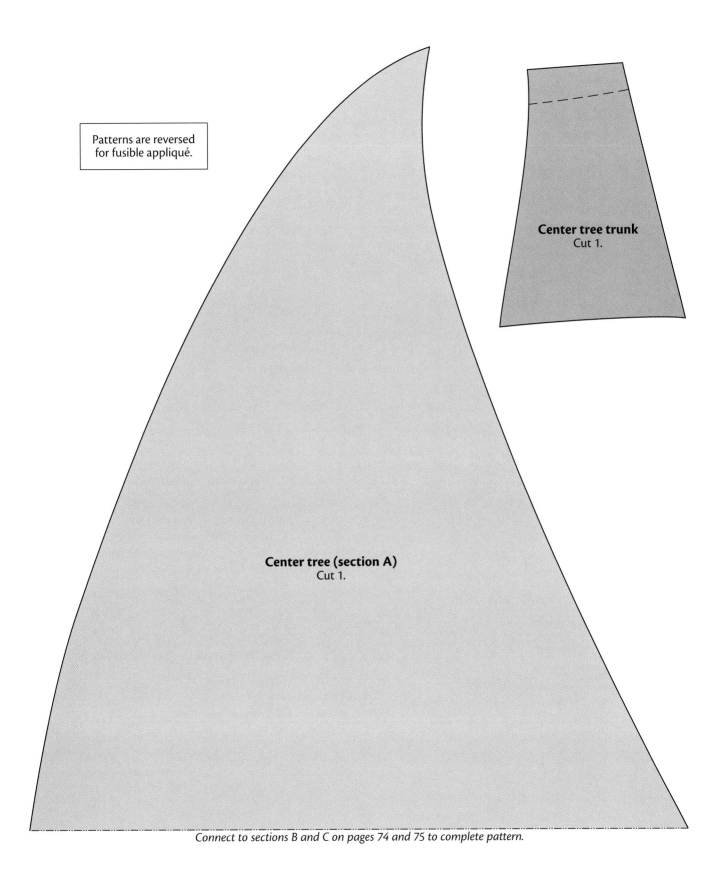

Patterns are reversed
for fusible appliqué.

Center tree trunk
Cut 1.

Center tree (section A)
Cut 1.

Connect to sections B and C on pages 74 and 75 to complete pattern.

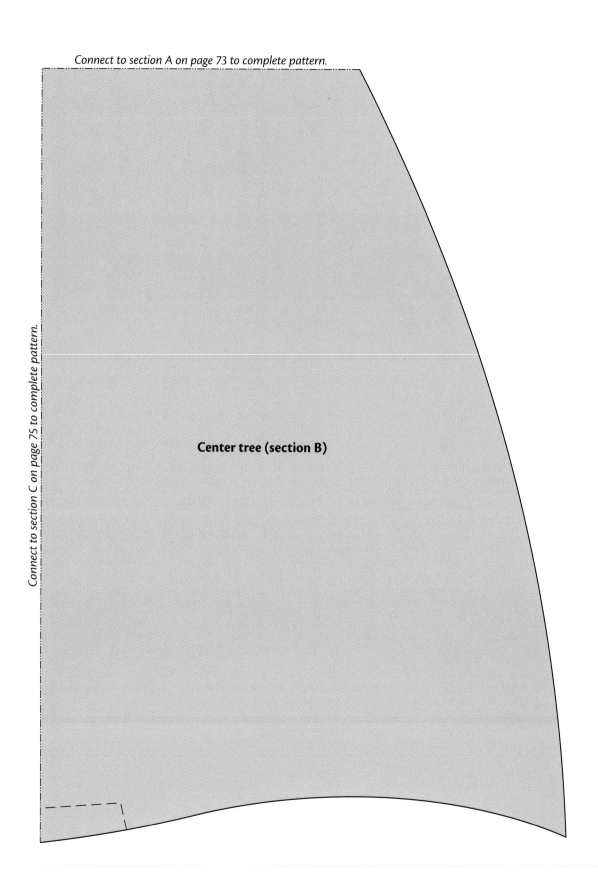

Connect to section A on page 73 to complete pattern.

Connect to section C on page 75 to complete pattern.

Center tree (section B)

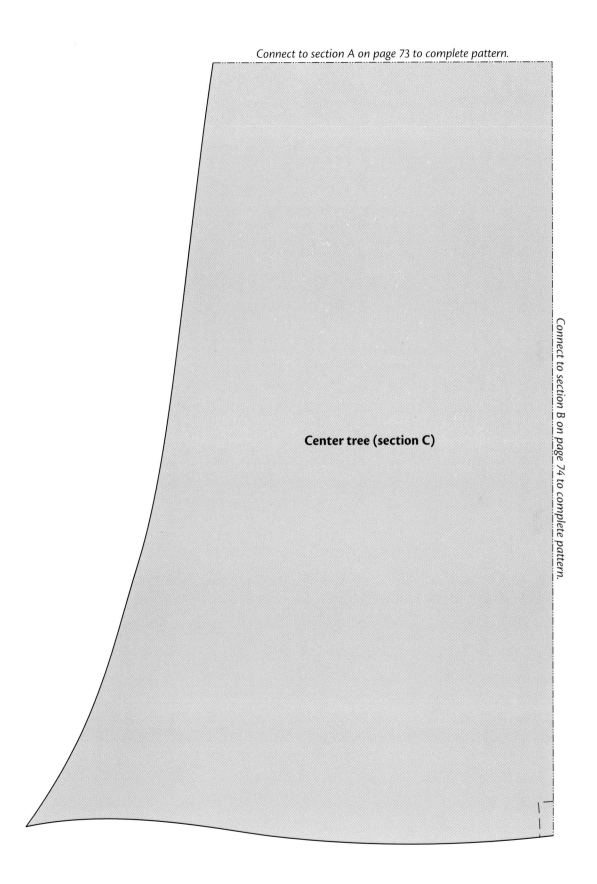

Connect to section A on page 73 to complete pattern.

Center tree (section C)

Connect to section B on page 74 to complete pattern.

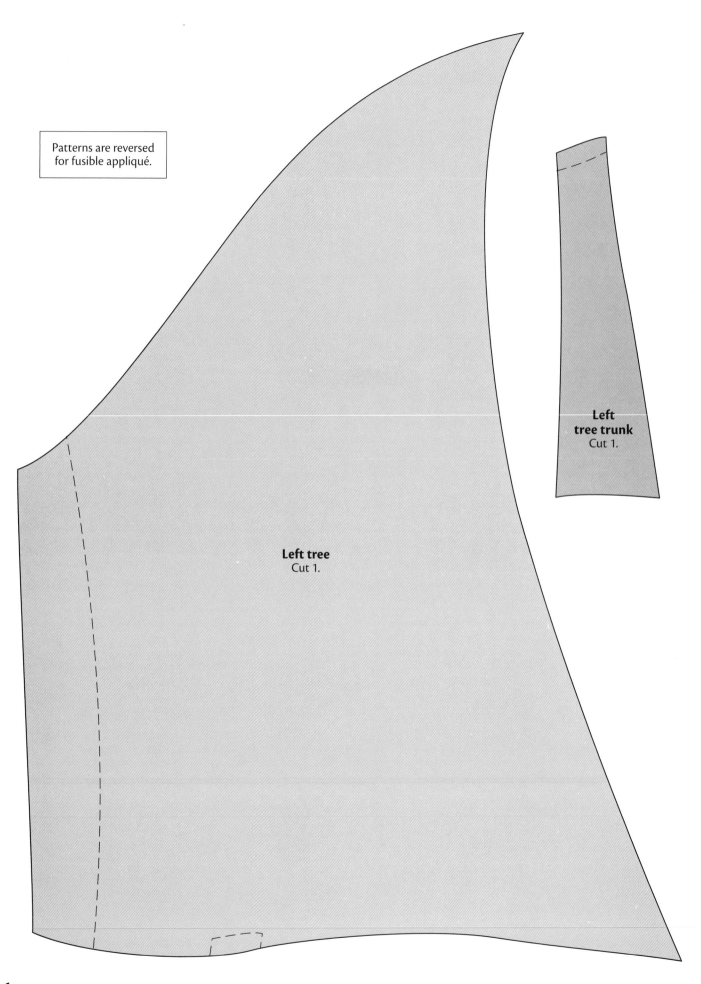

Patterns are reversed for fusible appliqué.

Left tree
Cut 1.

Left tree trunk
Cut 1.

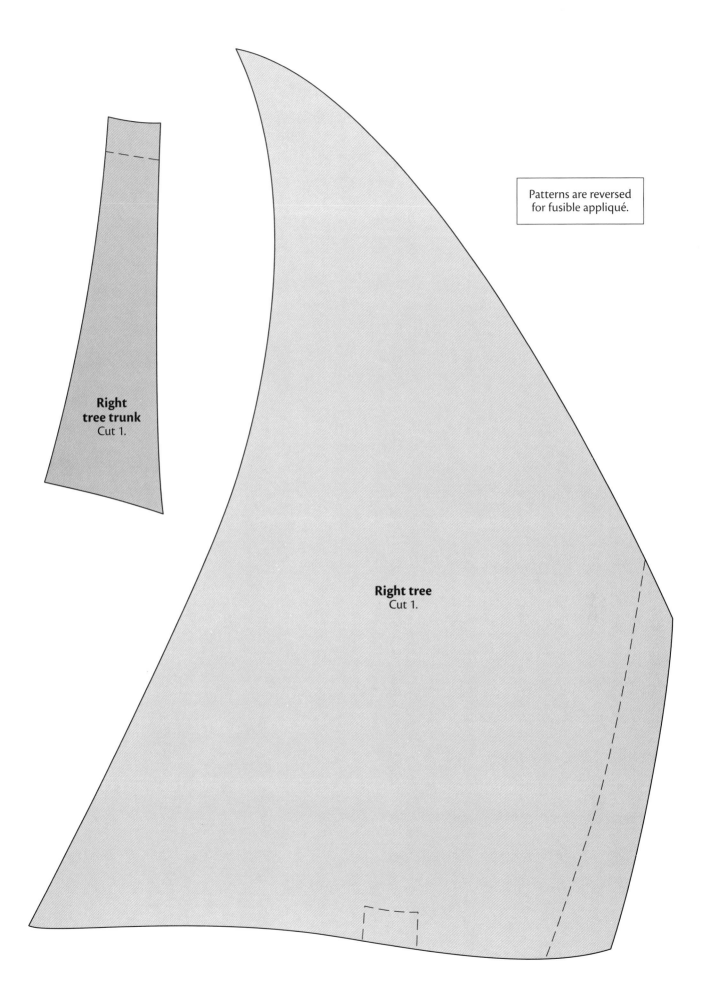

**Right
tree trunk**
Cut 1.

Right tree
Cut 1.

Patterns are reversed
for fusible appliqué.

about the author

Lisa MacDonald, Shutter Magik

LESLEY CHAISSON lives in Alberta, Canada, and is inspired by the changing landscapes from the Rocky Mountains to the plains. She and her husband, Colin, have four children: Maranelle, Teancum, Carter, and Haylee.

Lesley began sewing at age 8 and, despite her parents' suggestion to "start small," made her first quilt at age 14. Putting quilting aside for a few years, she started her own wedding-planning business, sewing bridesmaid dresses and wedding gowns. It wasn't until moving to northeastern Alberta and being inspired by her friend Trena that she indulged in quilting and joined the local quilt guild. She continues to design quilt patterns for her business, and you can contact her at www.candycornerquilting.com.

New and Best-Selling Titles from

APPLIQUÉ
Applique Quilt Revival
Beautiful Blooms
Cutting-Garden Quilts
Dream Landscapes
Easy Appliqué Blocks—NEW!
Simple Comforts—NEW!
Sunbonnet Sue and Scottie Too

BABIES AND CHILDREN
Baby's First Quilts
Baby Wraps
Let's Pretend
Snuggle-and-Learn Quilts for Kids
Sweet and Simple Baby Quilts

BEGINNER
Color for the Terrified Quilter
Happy Endings, Revised Edition
Machine Appliqué for the Terrified Quilter
Your First Quilt Book (or it should be!)

GENERAL QUILTMAKING
Adventures in Circles
American Jane's Quilts for All Seasons
Bits and Pieces
Bold and Beautiful—NEW!
Cool Girls Quilt
Country-Fresh Quilts
Creating Your Perfect Quilting Space
Fig Tree Quilts: Fresh Vintage Sewing—NEW!
Folk-Art Favorites—NEW!
Follow-the-Line Quilting Designs
    Volume Three
Gathered from the Garden
The New Handmade
Points of View
Prairie Children and Their Quilts
Quilt Revival
A Quilter's Diary, Written in Stitches
Quilter's Happy Hour
Quilting for Joy
Remembering Adelia—NEW!

Simple Seasons
Skinny Quilts and Table Runners
That Patchwork Place® Quilt Collection— NEW!
Twice Quilted
Young at Heart Quilts

HOLIDAY AND SEASONAL
Christmas Quilts from Hopscotch
Comfort and Joy
Holiday Wrappings

HOOKED RUGS, NEEDLE FELTING, AND PUNCHNEEDLE
Miniature Punchneedle Embroidery
Needle-Felting Magic
Needle Felting with Cotton and Wool

PAPER PIECING
Easy Reversible Vests, Revised Edition
Paper-Pieced Mini Quilts
Show Me How to Paper Piece
Showstopping Quilts to Foundation Piece
A Year of Paper Piecing

PIECING
501 Rotary-Cut Quilt Blocks
Favorite Traditional Quilts Made Easy
Loose Change
Maple Leaf Quilts
Mosaic Picture Quilts
New Cuts for New Quilts
Nine by Nine
On-Point Quilts
Quiltastic Curves
Ribbon Star Quilts
Rolling Along

QUICK QUILTS
40 Fabulous Quick-Cut Quilts
Instant Bargello
Quilts on the Double
Sew Fun, Sew Colorful Quilts
Supersize 'Em!—NEW!

SCRAP QUILTS
Nickel Quilts
Save the Scraps
Scrap-Basket Surprises—NEW!
Simple Strategies for Scrap Quilts
Spotlight on Scraps

CRAFTS
A to Z of Sewing—NEW!
Art from the Heart
The Beader's Handbook
Card Design
Crochet for Beaders
Dolly Mama Beads
Embellished Memories
Friendship Bracelets All Grown Up
Making Beautiful Jewelry
Paper It!
Trading Card Treasures

KNITTING & CROCHET
365 Crochet Stitches a Year
365 Knitting Stitches a Year
A to Z of Knitting
All about Knitting
Amigurumi World
Beyond Wool
Cable Confidence
Casual, Elegant Knits
Crocheted Pursenalities
Gigi Knits…and Purls
Kitty Knits
Knitted Finger Puppets
The Knitter's Book of Finishing
    Techniques
Knitting Circles around Socks
Knitting with Gigi
More Sensational Knitted Socks
Pursenalities
Simple Stitches—NEW!
Toe-Up Techniques for Hand-Knit
    Socks, Revised Edition
Together or Separate

Our books are available at bookstores and your favorite craft, fabric, and yarn retailers. If you don't see the title you're looking for, visit us at **www.martingale-pub.com** or contact us at:

1-800-426-3126
International: 1-425-483-3313
Fax: 1-425-486-7596 • **Email:** info@martingale-pub.com